IMAGES
of America

New York State Police Troop K

I0792588

Troop K Lamppost. This is the last remaining historic lamp from the Hawthorne Castle, Troop K Headquarters, located in Hawthorne. Now at the present headquarters site at Salt Point, the lamps were originally located at the entrance to the beautiful grounds of this historic structure used as Troop K's headquarters and illustrate the grand opulence that once represented the Hudson Valley's finest. It is also the officially designated logo for the recently formed Troop K Heritage Foundation.

On the cover: **GEDNEY FARMS, 1917.** Troopers head out for patrol from Troop K headquarters at Gedney Farms, White Plains, New York. (Author's collection.)

IMAGES
of America

NEW YORK STATE POLICE TROOP K

Frank Goderre

ARCADIA
PUBLISHING

ISBN 978-0-7385-4982-8

Published by Arcadia Publishing
Charleston, South Carolina

Printed in the United States of America

Library of Congress Control Number: 2006938006

For all general information, please contact Arcadia Publishing:
Telephone 843-853-2070
Fax 843-853-0044
E-mail sales@arcadiapublishing.com
For customer service and orders:
Toll-Free 1-888-313-2665

Visit us on the Internet at www.arcadiapublishing.com

Contents

Acknowledgments

The Troop K Heritage Foundation approved the selection of photographs submitted by present and former members of the New York State Police and the archives of the Peekskill Museum and the Van Cortlandtville Historical Society. The following sources have kindly provided material for this book: the New York State Police; Troop K; the archives of the *Peekskill Evening Star*; Lt. Donald P. Pagani (NYPD); Sgt. Daniel H. Snyder (1926–1938); and the families of trooper Albert Vitolo (1926–1938) and trooper Joseph Hunt (1926–1948). Thanks to the Village of Buchanan and Pete Lazaro for the vintage Theodore Roosevelt images. A special note of thanks to 1st Sgt. L. E. Moore for the support and encouragement that he extended to the author during the preparation of this project.

INTRODUCTION

The coming of the Industrial Revolution brought many changes to New York's Hudson Valley region. With improved highways and transportation means, inner-city crime had found its way into the rural areas of New York State. The traditional forms of justice proved to be inadequate for the rural communities.

The Empire State would still be debating a solution were it not for a tragedy that took place in the town of Bedford in Westchester County. Samuel Howell, a building foreman on the home that was being constructed for M. Moyca Newell, was attacked and shot seven times by four assailants while he was carrying the payroll and murdered. The four assailants escaped and were never captured, proving sheriff/constable law enforcement to be ineffective in dealing with such crimes.

Katherine Mayo and Moyca Newell launched a five-year campaign for a state constabulary, which would be responsible for all of New York's citizens in the rural areas of the state. This was a gigantic feat at a time when it was unlawful for females to vote in the general election process of this country. Through their untiring efforts, on March 17, 1917, with a bare majority in its favor, the Mills State Constabulary Bill, introduced by Sen. Ogden L. Mills, was passed by the Senate.

Gov. Charles P. Whitman turned to his old friend Maj. George Fletcher Chandler on his return home to Kingston from the Mexican border, where he served in the New York State National Guard. A meeting was held in the governor's office along with ex-president Theodore Roosevelt, and with the insistence of both men, Major Chandler accepted this herculean task.

Major Chandler immediately set out to form four troops throughout the state from the New York State National Guard, filling their ranks from existing units to form Troops A, D, G and K. By the authority of the secretary of war, 51 soldiers in federal service were discharged to the new state units "in the interest of public service." All appointed officers came directly from 1st New York Cavalry units throughout the state.

The 2nd Battalion, 11th Regiment of Artillery, New York Militia, had voted to rename itself the Battalion of National Guards in 1824 in tribute to the Marquis de Lafayette's *Garde Nationale*, honoring Lafayette's command of the Paris Militia. New York, by state statute, adopted the term *national guard* for its militia during the Civil War. The term was not recognized as the militia's formal title by federal legislation until the 1916 National Defense Act. Cavalry units were historically not only the first in battle but also the best. Major Chandler applied this principle of cavalrymen to be New York State's finest.

Major Chandler applied world history and New York State history in the establishment of this new organization, as indicated by this excerpt from his book, *The Policeman's Art*: "Law is supreme, and therefore the enforcement of the law or the maintenance of law is of the greatest importance in civilization. To maintain law or rules, monarchs or kings had only the men who fought to act as agents. The soldier, therefore, was the original policeman." This agent form of police work became the foundation by which the New York State troopers forever changed the rural scenery across the state and the Hudson Valley. Some 90 years later, the New York State Police is the only existing law enforcement agency in this country whose members do not display their shields on their headgear or uniforms, because they are "cavalrymen."

—Frank Goderre
Troop K Heritage Foundation

Troopers Leaving Troop Headquarters. Troopers leave headquarters, Gedney Farms in White Plains, to patrol the Hudson Valley region, including all of Long Island. The photograph was taken around 1918.

Col. Theodore Roosevelt and Troop K 1st U.S. Volunteer Cavalry. Troopers led by Col. Theodore Roosevelt, bottom right, patrol toward the state camp at Peekskill, now known as Camp Smith. This 1898 view is within 1,000 yards of the present state police Cortlandt station in the Crugers section of the town of Cortlandt.

One

The Formative Years, 1917–1929

Upon completion of training at Camp Newayo (a tribute to Moyca Newell and Katherine Mayo), the Troop D Farm in Manlius (the former home of Troop D, First New York Cavalry, National Guard), all 237 officers and men left for Syracuse to police the New York State Fair. When the fair ended, all four troops proceeded to their new headquarters. It took almost a month to transport all the personnel and equipment for Troop K.

On March 3, 1924, during a severe storm, fire struck Troop K's Gedney Farms at White Plains and destroyed it. All records, horses, and equipment were saved, but the barracks had to be relocated to the Hillandale Farm in New Rochelle and the offices were moved to the White Plains Armory until the new Troop K buildings were completed next to the Bronx River Parkway Extension at Hawthorne in Westchester County.

The patrol responsibility of Troop K embraced Nassau, Suffolk, Westchester, Putnam, Dutchess, Rockland, and Orange Counties. When Maj. George Fletcher Chandler envisioned and instituted the Department of State Police, he bestowed upon Troop K the challenge to enhance and modernize procedures and equipment throughout the state up until the early 1970s. Troop K held the honor of the most members promoted to superintendent, the highest rank in the New York State Police.

Here is a brief history of Troop K from its beginnings to the postwar era and the building of the most beautiful police structure in the world.

HISTORIC GEDNEY FARMS. This was the first Troop K Headquarters. Located in White Plains, it is pictured here in November 1917. The original stables of the Gedney family were transformed into quarters for the Hudson Valley cavalrymen. A total of 58 troopers assigned to

this installation included a captain, lieutenant, 1st sergeant, four duty sergeants, four corporals, a farrier, and a blacksmith. The location was used by the troopers until March 1924, when a tragic fire destroyed the building.

UNIFORM BUILDING STANDARDS. The Fearon Bill became law on April 26, 1921, adding two troops to the department—Troop B, Malone, and Troop C, Sidney. All troop headquarters buildings became uniform in architecture except for Troop K's, which remained distinct from those of other troops up until the early 1970s.

OFFICERS OF TROOP K. Capt. Ray D. Richman, first commander of Troop K, was replaced shortly after its first year by Capt. John A. Warner (center), pictured with his second in command, Lt. Eugene C. Roberts, and 1st Sgt. Francis McGarvey (right). Captain Warner succeeded Maj. George Fletcher Chandler and became the division's longest serving superintendent, from 1924 to 1944.

MEMBERS OF TROOP K. Troop K assembles for a photograph in front of the Gedney Farms headquarters. In front are Lieutenant Roberts, Captain Warner, and 1st Sergeant McGarvey.

STATE POLICE UNIFORMS. Pictured are uniforms of the New York State Police. From left to right are lieutenant's, sergeant's, and trooper's—full dress summer, field dress winter, full dress winter, and stables.

Trooper James Flynn Arrest. J. J. Broughton was arrested at Bay Shore, Long Island, on July 10, 1920, by trooper James Flynn of Troop K. Charged with forgery first degree, Broughton was sentenced to Sing Sing Prison on the Hudson River in Ossining.

Streetcar Strike. Shown is a picket line for a 1917 streetcar strike at the state armory in Buffalo. Seen here are, from left to right, trooper Robert J. Hackett, trooper Knudsen, trooper Bell, trooper Fowler, and trooper Bock.

"JACK DEMPSEY" OF TROOP K. Trooper Andy Grimes (left) and a fellow trooper are pictured with their Phaeton police cruisers. Trooper Grimes was routinely compared to famed boxer Jack Dempsey and was probably the largest trooper assigned to Troop K.

MAJ. GEORGE F. CHANDLER. Maj. George F. Chandler (dark suit) meets with his troop commanders at the capital offices in Albany.

EARLY TRANSPORTATION. Troopers prepare for patrol in their modern Ford Phaeton patrol cars. The cars were preferred over horses when time was of the essence in emergency troop movement around the state.

SIDECARS. Early motorcycle transportation included sidecars that routinely did not last long. This scene is the 1920 streetcar strike in the Albany-Troy area.

Capt. John A. Warner. John A. Warner, second from left, was Troop K commander from 1918 to 1923. Flanking him are inspector Lt. Albert B. Moore, left, and Lt. Harold J. Nagell of Troop G.

Trooper Chester A. Gilbert. Chester A. Gilbert entered the New York State Police on July 1, 1921, after serving in the Marine Corps in World War I. Placed in Troop K, Gilbert was promoted to sergeant in 1924 and became assistant director of the newly formed New York State School for Police. He resigned in 1927 and became a police officer for the town of Cortlandt. He is shown with his special partner who has donned his Stetson.

CAPT. JOHN M. KEELEY. John M. Keeley served as Troop K commander from 1923 to 1927. He was at Gedney Farms when it was heavily damaged by fire on March 3, 1924. Captain Keeley then temporarily moved the headquarters into the White Plains Armory.

CAPT. ELIHU F. TOBEY. Elihu F. Tobey, far right, was an original camp man from Troop A. He served as Troop K commander from 1927 to 1928, when he abruptly resigned from the state police. Pictured with him at the newly formed New York State School for Police in Troy are, from left to right, Lt. Harold J. Nagell, Col. George F. Chandler, Chief Wood (Kingston), and Lt. George P. Dutton.

GEDNEY FARMS FIRE. On March 3, 1924, during a severe storm, fire struck the Gedney Farms premises. There was no water available to fight the flames. Two unidentified troopers are shown inspecting the destroyed building.

Sergeant Gilbert. Sgt. Chester A. Gilbert is shown at the Monroe Substation in 1926.

Mineola Fair Detail. Troop K's Mineola Fair detail on Long Island, under the supervision of Lt. E. Hegeman, is seen here in September 1926.

GEDNEY FARMS HOTEL. On the same site as the Gedney Farms installation stood the famed Gedney Farms Hotel, which suffered a similarly tragic loss from fire on September 22, 1924. In the absence of water to contain the blaze, it also was destroyed. Note the architectural design of the structure, which may have played a role in the design of the future Troop K facility in Hawthorne.

RHINEBECK FAIR DETAIL. This is the Troop K contingent assigned to the 1927 Rhinebeck Fair.

State Police Monroe. This photograph shows Troop K, State Police Monroe in 1926. They are, from left to right, troopers Charles Mills, Harold VanDuzer, E. Stemmler, George Robinson, Sgt. Chester (Chick) Gilbert, George Searles, Harry Klein, Ed Haviland, Rodney Brown, and Joe McCure. In the background are their patrol vehicles and one mount.

State Police Monroe Substation. Two substations were added to the main headquarters in White Plains by adding State Police Monroe on the west side of the Hudson and State Police Brewster to handle the eastern side in the early 1920s.

Capt. Harold J. Nagell. Captain Nagell was the Troop K commander from July 1, 1928, to April 25, 1933. He joined the state police in 1917 and was made a corporal the following year. In 1919, he was promoted to sergeant. He was made a lieutenant in 1920 and, in July 1928, was made captain of the Westchester Division, Troop K. He was largely responsible for the construction of the new Troop K buildings on the Bronx Parkway Extension in Hawthorne. This became the highlight for New York City visionary and architect Robert Moses in addressing the growing traffic concerns on the newly constructed parkway system in Westchester County. All the parkways would point to the direction of this new public safety facility. At the time, it was considered the most modern highway system in the country.

HILLANDALE FARM. While personnel and equipment were at the White Plains Armory, the mounted horses were kept at the stables of the Hillandale Farm, located in New Rochelle.

STATE POLICE FISHKILL. Troopers Robbie, Buckley, Frandsen, and Gilbert (from left to right) were assigned to traffic detail in 1923.

Meal Time. Troop K troopers prepare a fire to make their hearty meal out in the rural patrol area.

Mounted Patrol. On horseback, troopers Shields and A. O'Connor patrol Kings Park, Long Island, in April 1926.

OVERCOMING POLITICS. With Maj. George Fletcher Chandler away, Governor Whitman lost the gubernatorial election to reform candidate Alfred E. Smith, a Democratic assemblyman who for two years led a bitter fight against the formation of a state police organization in New York. Major Chandler soon convinced the new governor otherwise, and Governor Smith told Major Chandler to make the New York State Police the best in the United States. Major Chandler's successor as superintendent, John A. Warner from Troop K, outdid Chandler by marrying the governor's daughter, pictured here. Governor Smith even had a castle built in Hawthorne for the members of Troop K.

Two

THE PROGRESSIVE YEARS, 1930–1940

Troop K experienced numerous changes in the next decade. Construction of the new Hawthorne headquarters was completed in late 1929, and the transfer of men, horses, motor vehicles and equipment from the White Plains Armory began on November 14, 1929. The formal dedication came a year later on November 15, 1930, with the Honorable Robert Moses and the presentation of a tree from Amawalk Nurseries.

Bloodhounds were assigned and housed at Troop K under the watchful eye of trooper W. W. Horton. The Bureau of Criminal Investigation was also added at this time. Radio transmitters were placed in service to provide reception only; later came the installation of two-way radio sets in troop vehicles, a first in the state. Troop K aviation started at the Armonk Airport in Westchester County. The first enclosed patrol cars were put in service along with a special black-and-white color scheme. A special traffic enforcement detail was provided for the parkways and highways.

The Division of State Police made its longest stride ever in the field of communications when the state police teletype system was installed, linking the states of New York, New Jersey, and Pennsylvania. On October 15, 1931, Gov. Franklin D. Roosevelt tapped out the first message from the Hawthorne barracks, officially putting the system into operation.

Providing security for Governor Roosevelt at his home in Hyde Park and throughout New York became a routine task for Troop K members that followed him into his presidential years. There existed a strong bond between Roosevelt and the contingent of troopers providing for his comfort and safety.

Troopers still had to contend with the Great Depression, joblessness, and illegal alcohol. Their workload continued to increase, with still little time off and extremely low pay. Duty hours were still 24-7 with two pass days allowed per month. It became increasingly hard for troopers to have a normal family life.

WHITE PLAINS ARMORY. From April 1924 to November 1929, the White Plains Armory served as the temporary headquarters of Troop K.

TROOP K HAWTHORNE UNDER CONSTRUCTION. Troopers anxiously awaited completion so they could move into their new permanent home. The architect for the castle, Sullivan Jones, had a flair for grand scale, and there existed in this building a resemblance to the grand opulence of the Gedney Farms Hotel. For many years to come, this building was known as the most beautiful police station in the world.

MOVING DAY. In this image, Hawthorne Barracks are now ready for occupancy. New York City architect Sullivan Jones followed the inspiration of the unforgettable beautiful buildings that once housed the troopers at Gedney Farms and the Gedney Farms Hotel that tragically burned in 1924. The dedication a year later included renowned New York City visionary Robert Moses and the two grand ladies who were the sole inspiration for the creation of the Department of State Police, Moyca Newell and Katherine Mayo, who served as hostesses at the dedication.

AERIAL VIEW, TROOP K HAWTHORNE. Beautiful and spacious quarters were provided for the Hudson Valley cavalrymen. Note the beautiful flower garden in the center courtyard shaped into the New York State Police shield. Nowhere in the country did a more beautiful and lavish

police facility compare with the Hawthorne headquarters. This building was completed in the same year the Great Depression took its toll on the country and gave rise to the great labor force that was instrumental in its construction.

TROOP K OFFICERS. Troop K commander Capt. Harold J. Nagell (left) and his second in command, Lt. Christopher Kemmler, are seen outside the new facility, looking quite pleased with their new home.

COURTYARD GARDENS. The most beautiful shrubs and flowers accent the main courtyard and front entrance of the castle.

Kitchen at the Castle. The well-equipped modern kitchen facilities of Troop K came with a professional chef and crew. No one appeared to starve with these modern conveniences.

Dining Hall at the Castle. This is the dining room for troopers and officers of Troop K; even the furniture is first class. Note the old schoolhouse lighting in the ceiling.

COMMUNICATIONS ROOM. Sgt. Daniel H. Snyder sits at the main desk of the communications room in the lobby of Troop K headquarters.

DAY ROOM. A separate day room for troopers to unwind and relax is depicted here. The furnishings represent a lavish setting that is appropriate to the castle style of architecture.

TACK ROOM. The well-laid-out tack room of the attached stables was extremely neat and clean. A well-earned trophy is on the center table.

TELETYPE ROOM. The teletype room of Troop K tapped out its first message to New Jersey and Pennsylvania on September 15, 1931. This communication system was used up until the early 1970s.

FOYER ENTRANCE. The elegant two-seat bench and clock stand in the foyer entrance. They have been preserved in the New York State Police Academy in Albany.

TACONIC STATE PARKWAY. Troopers stand by awaiting the arrival of Gov. Franklin D. Roosevelt in dedicating the Taconic State Parkway spur from Hawthorne north into Dutchess County in this image.

CHEVROLET PHAETON. Trooper Albert Vitolo completes his entries in a 1931 Chevrolet Phaeton convertible. These open-top vehicles were the staple of the fleet and actually gave better handling than closed sedans of that era. It was mandatory for the top to be down except in extremely bad weather and the transporting of prisoners. One cannot miss seeing the snow and the tire chains on the rear tires. Heavy sheepskin coats and hats protected troopers against the cold. This is the last of the unmarked black vehicles in the fleet.

EARLY FILE 3. This gray Phaeton convertible is actually a Troop K fleet vehicle, possibly a 1933 Chevrolet, involved in a File 3, a term used by state police personnel for division accidents. From the looks of the windshield, the trooper apparently was hurt. There were no seat belts of any kind back in the early days of motoring.

ROOSEVELT'S SECURITY DETAIL. Sgt. Earl Miller with Governor Roosevelt and Eleanor Roosevelt are seen here at a reception for foreign ambassadors in Albany. Formal dress presented a departure for the sergeant with the wearing of a white shirt and riding boots. It was widely rumored that Sergeant Miller and Eleanor were having an affair that had been going on for years.

ROOSEVELT'S SWIMMING EXERCISE. Sergeant Miller and the governor enjoy some time out exercising in the pool at Hyde Park.

HORSEBACK RIDING. Governor Roosevelt and Eleanor enjoy the trails of the Hyde Park estate with Sergeant Miller as escort.

CORNERSTONE DEDICATION. Governor Roosevelt is seen here with his security detail troopers at a Long Island park dedication and the laying of the cornerstone.

GOVERNOR'S LAUNCH. Shown here are Sgt. Earl Miller, trooper Walter Ellsroth, and the ship's captain aboard the governor's launch on Lake Champlain. Trooper Ellsroth completed a two-year enlistment, and his three sons, Thomas, Walter, and John, followed his footsteps in the 1950s by joining this elite group of police officers.

Heckscher Park Dedication. Attending the dedication of a state park on Long Island are troopers Rodney Brown, middle, and William Hamblin with Mr. Heckscher.

Sgt. Daniel H. Snyder. Daniel H. Snyder was known as the "Errol Flynn of the New York State Police." Interviewed in 1998 at the age of 94, he left listeners in amazement at his achievements while he was a New York State trooper from 1926 through 1938. There was little this member did not accomplish. He rode a horse, drove cars and motorcycles, and flew the Troop K plane from the Armonk Airport. His aviation wings are attached to his blouse.

TROOP K AVIATION. Sgt. Daniel H. Snyder prepares the plane for a mission from the airport in Armonk in Westchester County. The aviation detail was short-lived. A tragic plane crash took the lives of Lt. Tremain Hughes and his copilot, trooper Theophlius Gaines, when the fleet biplane struck an elm tree while on a mission, crashed, and burned in the town of Fenner in Madison County in 1932.

Troop K Aviation Pilots. Sergeant Snyder (left) and Cpl. Douglas Bock return from a flight to Long Island. Both troopers were seasoned pilots and saddened by the ending of the detail. Aviation did not return to the state police until the late 1960s, when the Thruway Detail started using planes on the New York State Thruway.

The Three Musketeers. Sgt. Charles LaForge, trooper Albert Vitolo, and trooper Joe Hunt (from left to right) enjoy a moment together in front of the Hawthorne Castle. All three members joined the New York State Police in the late 1920s and remained friends forever.

Dinner Bell. Sitting on the new State Police Hawthorne porch waiting for the dinner bell in 1930 are, from left to right, (first row) troopers Garland Blair and Frank Dwyer, Cpl. John J. Quinn (later deputy chief inspector), and 1st Sgt. Herschel Gay; (second row) Cpl. Daniel H. Snyder and troopers Vincent Dunn, Dan Kormandy, and Albert Vitolo.

Troop K Marriage Racket. Off on his honeymoon with his bride, Monica Lynch, trooper Albert Vitolo was assigned with other members of Troop K to a milk strike in Upstate New York in August 1931. No doubt Vitolo's leave request was denied by the Troop K commander.

Milk Strike. Union milk strikes in Upstate New York plagued the New York State Police in the 1930s.

PRIMITIVE HIGHWAY CONDITIONS. Troopers had to overcome poor safety markings causing an abundance of railroad crossing accidents. Here Cpl. John J. Quinn (left) and trooper Douglas Bock investigate a Hearn-owned truck at Valhalla in July 1931. The Depression actually helped modernize New York State roadways through the 1930s, with federal Works Progress Administration (WPA) monies that were used to upgrade many of the highways. Concrete replaced many of the dirt and gravel roadways.

TRAIN VERSUS TANKER. A Standard Oil Company tanker was struck by the No. 26 Albany-New York Express just south of Newburgh on August 19, 1931. The wreckage is investigated by Troop K's Cpl. W. H. Hamblin and trooper Ernie Goodspeed of Cornwall.

TROOPER JOE HUNT. Troop K trooper Joe Hunt was the senior motor operator favored by Gov. Franklin D. Roosevelt in providing executive escorts throughout the state.

STANDARD-ISSUE PATROL CARS. Sgt. Daniel H. Snyder operates the department's Chevrolet Phaeton convertible in the early 1930s. The vehicle had no markings and was the standard gray color. The Phaetons were equipped with only a siren and no emergency lights. Regulations at the time required the top to be in the down position at all times for easy recognition of the troopers, which did not always work.

BAY SHORE DETAIL. Troopers Snyder and Martin are seen here at zone headquarters in Bay Shore, Long Island, in April 1932.

ZONE HEADQUARTERS, BAY SHORE. Troopers Snyder and Martin confer at the Main Street, Bay Shore, Long Island, zone headquarters. The station was a designated teletype station for receiving and sending teletype alerts throughout the state. It had two sergeants and five uniformed troopers to patrol a large section of Suffolk County.

City Trust Company Investigation. Sgt. Daniel H. Snyder confers with the Westchester County district attorney about the investigation of the robbery of the City Trust Company in 1931.

Rockland County Still Raid. Troopers shut down a bootlegging operation in Rockland County in August 1930. Seen here are, from left to right, troopers Carl Shaver, Irving Jagoda, C. Raven, Ed Wehmann, Dan Glasheen, and L. Degenhardt.

TROOPERS GUARD MAX BAER. Professional boxer Max Baer arrives in New York City for a match, with state troopers forming a guard of honor on September 3, 1935. His son is well-known actor Max Baer Jr., who played Jethro in the 1960s television series *The Beverly Hillbillies.*

TROOP K COMMANDER DIES. Troop K commander Capt. Harold James Nagell died on April 24, 1933. Here he lies in state at Troop K headquarters with Sgts. Charles LaForge (left) and Douglas Bock standing guard.

TROOP K SALUTE. Members of Troop K stand at attention and salute their fallen commander, Captain Nagell. Captain Nagell died on April 24, 1933, on the golf course of the Englewood County Club in Englewood, New Jersey, while playing in a tournament held by the Automobile Merchants Association of New York. Only 41 years old, he fell victim to a cerebral hemorrhage. He was a personal friend of John D. Rockefeller Jr. and made his home on the grounds of Rockefeller's Pocantico Hills estate. This was a tragic loss to the members of Troop K and the New York State Police.

COMMANDER'S FUNERAL. Troop K pallbearers carry their fallen commander, followed by his favorite mount, during the funeral procession.

FUNERAL PROCESSION. Troopers and area police officers stand at attention as the procession leaves the grounds of Troop K headquarters.

FITTING TRIBUTE. The funeral cortege awaits the pallbearer detail in this image. The fallen commander's boots are affixed rearward in the stirrups, in traditional ceremonial cavalry tradition. Capt. Harold Nagell was an original member of the New York State Police when it was formed in 1917. He proudly served in Troops D, G, and K and will be forever revered in the history of Troop K.

HEARSE. Capt. Harold Nagell's funeral procession, with his mount following the hearse, leaves the grounds of Troop K headquarters.

FUNERAL ROUTE. The funeral procession reaches the Bronx River Parkway, headed to the Harmon train station in Croton-on-Hudson to meet the train that will transport the beloved troop commander to his final resting place in his native Cortland.

Final Resting Spot. Captain Nagell's final service was held at the Hotel Dewey in Cortland and at his grave site in the Cortland Cemetery.

Shooting Range. Cpl. Sam J. Crodelle is seen here at the Troop K firing range. Extremely low pay, long work hours, and personnel layoffs were common in Troop K after seasonal summer workforce expansion and may explain the "taxpayer" silhouette on one of the targets.

TROOP K'S BUREAU OF CRIMINAL INVESTIGATION. Sgt. Daniel H. Snyder sits at his desk at the Hawthorne Barracks Bureau of Criminal Investigation. It was here that the bureau was formed and, through Sergeant Snyder, the simplified Henry system of fingerprint classification was implemented. Sergeant Snyder also instructed law enforcement personnel and troopers at the state police academy in Troy.

RYDER CIDER MILL MURDER CASE. Sgt. Charles A. LaForge solved the shocking murder of cider mill farmer William Ryder at a small farm in Yorktown Heights in February 1932 with the arrest and conviction of four assailants. From left to right are Sergeant LaForge, Cpl. Dan Glasheen, suspects Grant "Doc" Robertson, Edwin Johnson, Jack Kovel, and Tommy Jackson, and troopers Francis Kappesser, Samuel Crodelle, and Keily.

1st Sgt. Charles A. LaForge. This trooper symbolized some of the greatest achievements in making Troop K one of the best police agencies in the country. Countless felony arrests and convictions made the rural region the safest in the New York metropolitan area. His strong ethical views later put him in direct confrontations with two superintendents, resulting in a change in division policies.

Imitating Dillinger, Slayers. The August 8, 1935, murder of 23-year-old Raymond H. Pierce from Oscawana Corners sent Peter Mohlsick (second from left) and Howard Eichler (third from left) to the electric chair at Sing Sing after their arrest by Sgt. Charles LaForge and trooper Francis Kappesser. They intended to rob Pierce of his car and acted out the crime emulating their hero, John Dillinger. Mohlsick and Eichler were electrocuted at Sing Sing on April 16, 1936.

Maurigo Murder Case. Biaggia Marcucci was arrested by troopers W. W. Horton (left) and Gerald Dershiemer for the murder of Mario Maurigo.

TROOP K MOTOR UNIT. A motorcycle unit gets ready for patrol in this image. Motorcycles were primarily used for traffic enforcement. Unit members worked day tours only.

STILL RAID. Troopers Harold Galvin (left) and Steve Bugala seize a huge bootlegging operation in the town of Yorktown in May 1938.

TROOP COMMANDERS. Supt. John A. Warner is pictured here with his troop commanders at an Albany meeting. From left to right are Capt. James Flynn (Troop L), Babylon; Capt. W. W. Robinson (Troop A), Batavia; Capt. Christopher Kemmler (Troop K), Hawthorne; Capt. Charles Broadfield (Troop B), Malone; Chief Inspector A. B. Moore, Troy; Superintendent Warner; Capt. George Dutton, adjutant; Capt. Steve McGrath (Troop D), Oneida; Capt. Dan Fox (Troop C), Sidney; and Capt. Jack Keeley (Troop G), Troy. The majority of these commanders started with the New York State Police in 1917.

STILL RAID ARRESTS. Troopers Steve Bugala (left) and Harold Galvin are seen here with suspects from the raid on a still at Dr. West's farm in Shrub Oak in August 1938. They were processed in the village of Peekskill lockup.

SHRUB OAK STILL RAID. Troopers Harold Galvin and Steve Bugala raid an illegal still operating on Dr. West's property in Shrub Oak.

CAPTAIN KEMMLER DIES. Capt. Christopher Kemmler, commanding officer of Troop K, died of thrombosis on May 28, 1937, in his home at age 40. He was the second commander to die unexpectedly in a four-year span. He was named captain after the death of Capt. Harold Nagell. Both captains served as troop commander for four years in Troop K.

Captain Gaffney Named Troop K Commander. Capt. John A. Gaffney is sworn in as Troop K commander by Supt. John A. Warner. Captain Gaffney succeeded Captain Kemmler.

Peace Pipe. Capt. John A. Gaffney settles a dispute between saddler trooper Peter Burke (left) and groundskeeper Marshall and gets them to shake hands.

BERMUDA FUGITIVE. In the spring of 1938, 1st Sgt. Herschel A. Gay, at the request of the Nassau County district attorney's office, flies to Bermuda with Troop K's famed bloodhound in search of a fugitive.

NEW FLEET. Members of Troop K's traffic detail check out with Sgt. Irving Jagoda a new Harley Davidson delivered to the troop in the spring of 1938.

ROAD TEST. Trooper C. F. "Red" Ahern, on patrol in South Millbrook, checks out the new motorcycle.

BLACK-AND-WHITE PATROL CARS. This beautiful 1937 Phaeton being displayed by Sgt. Irving Jagoda is the first patrol car to feature the black-and-white color scheme, which was assigned exclusively to special traffic units. Note the steady red emergency light mounted on the left fenders of vehicles used by the special units.

Standard Patrol Cars. This gray, unmarked patrol vehicle was the standard in Troop K. This photograph was taken in the village of West Haverstraw in May 1939, the last year the Phaeton was used in service by the Division of State Police.

Reception-Only Radios. Troop K members adjust the antenna on the traffic unit. One-way radios—reception only—were used by the troop until the late 1930s.

TRAFFIC ASSIGNMENTS. 1st Sgt. E. J. Dougherty gives a traffic detail assignment to troopers Albert Vitolo and G. Dersheimer for patrolling Route 17 in Rockland and Orange Counties. This was the last year Troop K used the Phaetons (four-door convertibles) as its primary patrol vehicle. Prior to the 1930s, this model was considered to have the finest handling characteristics available; enclosed cars were too top-heavy and were prone to rolling over. These special highway vehicles came equipped with Ford's famous 85-horsepower flathead V-8 engines, also favored by legendary gangsters. The black-and-white vehicles were perfectly suited for high-speed traffic enforcement.

BCI VEHICLE. The Bureau of Criminal Investigation (BCI) utilized this 1937 Ford panel truck for crime scene investigations.

TROOP K PATROL VEHICLE. The gray, permanently marked 1939 Ford Deluxe became the staple of Troop K. Permanent markings first appeared on the 1938 units.

FORD WOODY PATROL CAR. Bloodhound handler Sgt. W. W. Horton is pictured with his 1938 Ford Woody wagon, which was used to track missing persons and fugitives from justice.

BLOODHOUND TRAILER. Trooper G. Dersheimer (left) and Sergeant Horton previously utilized a trailer towed by a patrol car to accommodate the bloodhounds for searches.

TROOP K PISTOL TEAM. Troop K's pistol team is photographed with Capt. John A Gaffney. Seen here are, from left to right, troopers Roberts, Hastings, Tom Dorr, W. W. Horton, and Herb Bergland. The team won numerous trophies for the troop.

SHIRLEY TEMPLE. Trooper Joe Hunt poses with famous child actress Shirley Temple.

Radio-Equipped Patrol Cars. New 1939 Chevrolet patrol vehicles were also equipped with the latest Link-manufactured two-way radio systems tuned to receive from the Nassau County Police radio system. Troop K was the first troop in the state to receive this modern equipment.

RADIO EQUIPMENT. Cpl. Harry Broadbent tests a new Harley Davidson motorcycle equipped with the latest technological advance—two-way radio systems—in preparation for the New York World's Fair in April 1939. The new motorcycles are barely distinguishable from other machines except for a small black loudspeaker mounted on the handlebars and two silver-colored cases containing the receiving equipment and batteries attached to each side of the rear wheel.

CRIME SPREE. Lester Brockelhurst, a 23-year-old former Illinois Sunday school teacher and paroled convict, and his accomplice, Bernice Felton, age 18, were wanted in three homicides and 23 robberies across 13 states. When trooper Joe Hunt stopped their car near Brewster on May 14, 1937, Felton pleaded with Brockelhurst not to kill the trooper, said she had had enough of the crime spree and urged him to give himself up. Hunt testified in a Little Rock, Arkansas, courtroom against Brockelhurst, who was executed two days later following the trial. Felton was spared execution.

ROYAL ESCORT. The Troop K motorcade receives assignments from Sgt. Irving Jagoda in preparation for the royal escort of King George VI and Queen Elizabeth of Great Britain from the New York World's Fair in New York City to Hyde Park as guests of Pres. Franklin D. Roosevelt on June 11, 1939. This was the first time the royal family visited the United States.

READY TO MOUNT. Troop K's motorcycle escort prepares to mount for the royal escort from the New York World's Fair to Hyde Park. Trooper Joe Hunt was the lead motor unit for the escort.

TROOP K SECURITY DETAIL. Troop K's trooper Tom Dorr (center) and two other members await the arrival of the royal family along the route at the Hawthorne Circle in Hawthorne. More than 150,000 people lined the route to Hyde Park to get a glimpse of the royal family.

TROOPER JOE HUNT, LEAD ESCORT. Troop K's veteran motorcycle operator trooper Joe Hunt, with the United States flag attached, leads the royal escort through the village of Peekskill on the Bear Mountain Parkway Extension, exiting at Highland Avenue and proceeding to Route 9 north to Hyde Park.

QUEEN WAVES TO PEEKSKILL FOLK. More than 5,000 people see royalty pass through the village of Peekskill and the town of Cortlandt as Queen Elizabeth waves to the excited crowd. Rain threatened as the royal family left Columbia University, so a closed limousine was substituted for an open car.

ROYAL FAMILY AND THE ROOSEVELTS. Here are Queen Elizabeth, King George VI, Pres. Franklin D. Roosevelt, and First Lady Eleanor Roosevelt at the Roosevelt estate in Hyde Park on June 11, 1939.

Royal Family Bound for Canada. Queen Elizabeth and King George VI are pictured aboard a train leaving Hyde Park for a trip north to Canada.

Thank You From the Secretary of State. Cordell Hull, Pres. Franklin D. Roosevelt's secretary of state, expressed thanks for the royal escort in a letter to Capt. John A. Gaffney. Secretary of State Hull noted that at no time during the entire movement of the royal train through New York State en route to Canada was the train out of sight of this marked patrol car and other vehicles of the New York State Police, which traveled on adjacent roadways.

ROLL CALL. Morning roll call and inspection at State Police Millbrook are depicted in this image. Lt. W. F. Reilly is the supervisor.

ENGRAVED DESK. This beautifully engraved desk is in the main radio room of the Bay Shore, Long Island, substation.

WINTRY SCENE. Troop K's Hawthorne Castle has a Currier and Ives quality after the first snowfall in December 1939. Scenes such as this provided Christmas cards for Troop K to send to fellow members and friends of the state police for years to come. The castle automatically took on a festive look in winter.

Three

The Turbulent Years, 1940–1949

With war clouds on the horizon, Troop K faced its greatest challenge in this decade. The United States had to help liberate Germany and Japan from their evil rulers and create a generation that would spread freedom and prosperity around the globe, while a handful of troopers kept New York's Hudson Valley safe and secure throughout the war years.

The United States and the people of the world looked to New York's former governor, Pres. Franklin D. Roosevelt, to lead them to victory. President Roosevelt's death in April 1945 brought sorrow and grief throughout the world, but it was a crushing blow to the members of Troop K, who had enjoyed a personal relationship with him for more than 20 years. Troop K also saw the departure of one of its own, Supt. John A. Warner, when he entered the service of his country in 1944 after serving the longest term of any superintendent in the history of the New York State Police.

The new generation from the 1940s also stood up to Stalin and his successors in spreading the new freedom and opposing communism. Troop K faced a communist challenge of its own in the form of an outdoor concert in the town of Cortlandt at the end of the summer in 1949 that became known as the Robeson Riots. The riots were escalated by local veterans groups opposed to the ideological views of the main performer, Paul Robeson, an avowed communist, especially because the concert took place close to numerous cemeteries that were interring casualties of World War II that were returning from Europe and the Pacific. Criticism of the Troop K troopers assigned to the concert persisted for years; the images on the following pages will present a different perspective. Newspaper and magazine reports and numerous pictures of the Robeson incident were part of a file used for study by the House of Representatives and Senate conferees of the 83rd Congress in preparation for the 1954 legislation to outlaw the Communist Party in the United States.

ACCIDENT AFTERMATH. This Troop K member faced the task of getting his Harley Davidson motorcycle repaired after an accident.

ORANGE COUNTY FAIR. Troopers Ed Lent (left) and Harry Nelson patrol the Orange County Fair in Middletown in the summer of 1940.

STATE POLICE MIDDLETOWN. This photograph shows Troop K Middletown barracks in the early 1940s. Seen here are, from left to right, Cpl. Jack Kohlsted, trooper Emmett Donohue, Lt. Dan Glasheen, trooper Charlie Hanzel, and investigator William Hamblin.

RADIO COMMUNICATIONS VEHICLE. With war clouds on the horizon and German submarines spotted off Long Island, state police purchased this mobile radio communications truck with a fully equipped trailer to monitor the threat from Germany.

Bear Mountain Bridge. State park commissioner Robert Moses won State Council of Parks approval to force the private owners of the Bear Mountain Bridge to sell the span to the state for $2.3 million in 1940. The toll was reduced to 50¢ from $2. Troop K members are shown at the official dedication of the state takeover of the first bridge to cross the Hudson below Albany. The bridge also gave access to the sprawling Bear Mountain Park, a gift from the Harriman family, which originally built the bridge through a private corporation in 1924.

BCI Evidence Vehicle. This 1941 Ford panel truck had to provide the Troop K BCI with long service because of World War II. No United States car manufacturer produced vehicles until the end of the war in 1945.

Ration Stickers. The ration sticker (A) is quite noticeable on trooper Benjamin Bailey's 1941 Chevrolet Deluxe sedan patrol car in Jefferson Valley in 1942. Fuel and tires were rare commodities with the war raging, and federal rationing became the law of the land.

BUCHANAN BARRACKS. Only two troopers were assigned to the Peekskill-Cortlandt area throughout the 1940s. Here are troopers Emmett Donohue (left) and Tom Darby, assigned to the Buchanan Barracks, village of Buchanan, town of Cortlandt.

STATE POLICE PORT JERVIS, ORANGE COUNTY. Trooper Ernie Goodspeed was the lone trooper assigned to the Port Jervis-Orange County area. When troopers needed assistance, backup officers were few and far between.

TRAFFIC UNITS. The 1941 black-and-white Fords of the special traffic unit were the last for some time. World War II halted all car production when the automobile manufacturers geared up for war production until 1945. This color scheme did not return to state police units until 1955. It then became the standard theme for all marked vehicles in division use for the next 19 years.

PLANE CRASH. Two young men ages 15 and 14 "borrowed" a 1940 red Continental monoplane from the Amityville Airport on Long Island on July 11, 1940, and were heading for Canada when they realized they were running low on fuel. They landed safely on the Wilkie Todd farm in the town of Cortlandt and refueled with four gallons from a local gas station but crashed on takeoff. Here trooper H. W. Boehack investigates the crash scene.

PLANE CRASH SUSPECTS. Bernard Byrne, 15, and Donald Blood, 14, of Massapequa, Long Island, are seen here at the city of Peekskill lockup with trooper Boehack, Chief Joseph Lillis, and patrolman Anthony Anastasi, the officer who found the young men enjoying themselves in a local swimming hole.

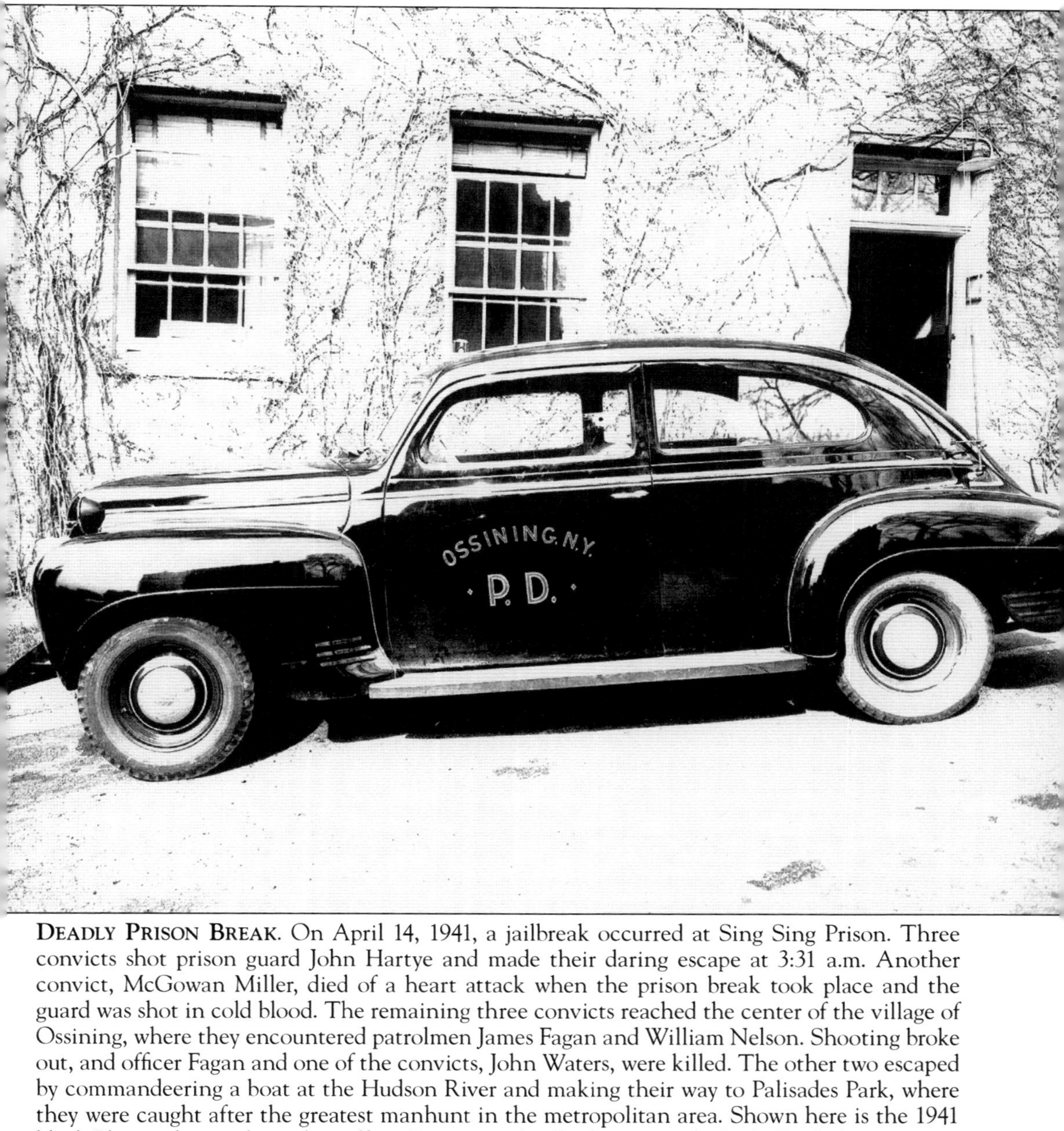

DEADLY PRISON BREAK. On April 14, 1941, a jailbreak occurred at Sing Sing Prison. Three convicts shot prison guard John Hartye and made their daring escape at 3:31 a.m. Another convict, McGowan Miller, died of a heart attack when the prison break took place and the guard was shot in cold blood. The remaining three convicts reached the center of the village of Ossining, where they encountered patrolmen James Fagan and William Nelson. Shooting broke out, and officer Fagan and one of the convicts, John Waters, were killed. The other two escaped by commandeering a boat at the Hudson River and making their way to Palisades Park, where they were caught after the greatest manhunt in the metropolitan area. Shown here is the 1941 black Plymouth patrol car that officer Fagan was fatally shot in, with the bullet hole appearing in the driver's door glass.

Getaway Car. This is the convicts' 1939 Plymouth sedan, which was parked at the Ossining train station with a machine gun and loaded with ammunition waiting for them. Mistakenly they approached the car that had officers James Fagan and William Nelson inside. The convicts' vehicle was being held for evidence at Troop K's headquarters in Hawthorne.

Search Team. Among the members of the largest search team were these two Ossining police officers and Sgt. W. W. Horton of Troop K. The prisoners were found and arrested eight hours after the escape and were taken to the Ossining Police Department lockup.

TROOP K BLOODHOUNDS. Sergeant Horton (left) and trooper Tom Darby work with the Troop K bloodhounds, which first joined Troop K in the early 1930s.

GOV. THOMAS E. DEWEY. Gov. Thomas E. Dewey of Pawling enjoys the safety and comfort of state police protection. Shown is Sgt. Francis G. Kappesser, head of the Governor's Detail, troopers assigned from the state police force to protect the governor and his family around the clock.

AROUND-THE-CLOCK SECURITY. Sgt. Francis Kappesser, second from left, and Sgt Albin S. Johnson, second from right, provide around-the-clock security for Gov. Thomas E. Dewey and his wife, Frances. Frances disliked the purple worn on troopers' uniforms, so plans were made to alter the color of the ties and hatband in 1954 when the uniforms were changed to a more modern design. The plans evaporated after W. A. Harriman was elected governor in 1954.

Governor Rides in Style. Sergeant Kappesser drives Governor Dewey, rear seat, to the Pawling train station in a luxury Buick convertible.

Governor's Mansion. Governor Dewey's Troop K security detail is pictured in front of the governor's home in Pawling. Sergeant Kappesser is on the left.

STATE POLICE GUARD SHACK. A far cry from the governor's home is this small shack to shield troopers from inclement weather on the governor's estate in Pawling.

CAMP SMITH. Gov. Thomas E. Dewey inspects the soldiers at Camp Smith New York State National Guard training camp in the town of Cortlandt with trooper Harold H. Galvin at the campsite in June 1943.

Troop K Pistol Team. 1st Sgt. John Lawson poses with Troop K's crack pistol team at the Teaneck, New Jersey, Northeast Pistol Matches in 1944.

Pistol Shooting Range. Troop K's Long Island pistol range was built by members of Troop L. The range was later handed back over to Troop K.

CHIEF INSPECTOR. Francis S. McGarvey is promoted to the rank of chief inspector by Supt. John A. Warner in Albany in 1944. McGarvey was the original Troop K camp man who began his career as a private in the New York State Police in July 1917. Chief inspector McGarvey became the fifth superintendent of state police and the fourth from Troop K.

PRESIDENTIAL FUNERAL. Troop K troopers assigned to Pres. Franklin D. Roosevelt's funeral await the train carrying the fallen chief executive at Hyde Park on April 26, 1945.

PRESIDENTIAL BURIAL SITE. Troop K members stand guard at President Roosevelt's grave site in Hyde Park in April 1946.

PRESIDENT TRUMAN. Pres. Harry S. Truman with Eleanor Roosevelt lays a wreath at the former president's burial site in Hyde Park.

GEN. CHARLES DEGAULLE. Provisional President of France Gen. Charles DeGaulle places a wreath in honor of the late president Franklin D. Roosevelt at the burial site in Hyde Park.

PRESIDENT ROOSEVELT'S SIDEKICK FALA. Even the late president's favorite sidekick, Fala, pays her last farewell to the commander in chief at his grave site.

BRITISH SECRETARY OF STATE. The British Secretary of State stands with 1st Sgt. R. F. Ficke at Roosevelt's funeral.

Roosevelt Presidential Funeral Detail. Capt. Daniel F. Glasheen, inspector Robert V. Annett, and Lt. Charles P. Curtain are seen here with members of Troop K honoring the late president Franklin D. Roosevelt at his residence in Hyde Park. This was a mournful time for the many members of Troop K who had become personally close to the former governor and then chief executive of the United States with immense pride to see a local New Yorker rise to be the leader of the free world.

FIVE-STAR GENERAL. Seen here is five-star general Dwight D. Eisenhower, under the watchful eye of Troop K's trooper Joe Hunt, at his arrival at West Point, near Highland Falls, in the summer of 1945. This was the man who did much to spread freedom and prosperity around the globe and liberate Germany and Japan.

GEN. DWIGHT D. EISENHOWER. Trooper Hunt is making sure the general and future president remains safe and secure while visiting West Point in the Hudson Valley in the summer of 1945.

TROOP K WORLD WAR II VETERAN. Troop K commander Capt. Daniel F. Glasheen is seen here congratulating trooper J. M. Brady (center) for his service to his country in Europe at West Point. At the ceremony are, from left to right, Lt. John J. Lawson, Deputy Supt. George M. Searle, Captain Glasheen, and Sgt. Alex Kormandy.

TROOP K PATROL UNITS. Following the war and the resumption of automobile manufacturing, orders for new cars were slow and choice of colors was not a priority. Any combination of colors was taken just to replace the aging fleet from 1942. Pictured here is a light-colored Ford deluxe sedan with its newly installed two-way radio system introduced in 1946 as standard division equipment.

Troop Two-Way Radios. A Troop K trooper displays the use of the new handheld two-way radio system installed in all division patrol vehicles starting in 1946.

Radio Transmitters. The early cumbersome two-way radio transmitters took up most of the trunk space in division patrol cars. Check out the added five-mile handheld flashlight that also became standard division equipment for years to come.

STATION TWO-WAY RADIO TRANSMITTERS. All troop headquarters and substations were equally equipped with the latest two-way radios, greatly improving police work around the troop and state. Trooper E. J. Svec at Bay Shore, Long Island, dispatches messages to members in the field in this image.

VETERAN SOLDIERS APPLY. Returning members of all branches of the service are taking the New York State trooper exam at White Plains under the guidance of trooper Herbie Stahn in 1946.

STOLEN PATROL CAR SUSPECT BOOKED. 1st Sgt. Albin S. Johnson books stolen police car suspect Richard Chapman at the Troop K headquarters in Hawthorne in May 1948. Standing guard are Cpl. Ray McCoy (left) and trooper Alvin Schaefer. Chapman and his accomplice, Dominick Lossacco, both of the Bronx, robbed Corporal McCoy of his own service revolver and patrol car on the Taconic Parkway near Route 6 in Shrub Oak after they thrust a .32 caliber automatic into his ribs when the corporal stopped to interview the pair. The pair then fled south on the parkway in the stolen patrol car. Receiving the radio message previously sent by Corporal McCoy, trooper Schaefer responded to the scene and picked up McCoy. An 80 m.p.h. pursuit quickly ended after McCoy, using Schaefer's .45 service revolver, returned fire at the fleeing patrol car, leaving Lossacco, the driver, with a wound to the face, causing the stolen patrol car to leave the highway and drive over an embankment, where both suspects were apprehended.

Taconic Pistol Duel. On May 20, 1948, Cpl. Raymond McCoy (left) and trooper Alvin Schaefer examine the stolen trooper car at troop headquarters. A police bullet entered the left rear door glass, striking Lossacco in the face, and proceeded through the left front section of the windshield.

Bullet-riddled Troop Car. At troop headquarters, Corporal McCoy's 1946 Ford patrol car is held for forensic tests after a running gun battle between two hoodlums in the stolen patrol car and troopers in hot pursuit. The good guys prevailed.

DUSTING FOR FINGERPRINTS. Sgt. C. B. VanAlen and an assistant dust a recovered stolen vehicle at troop headquarters in Hawthorne in 1948.

CROTON AIRPORT PLANE CRASH. Trooper James Cooney of State Police Buchanan and another trooper investigate a plane crash in the town of Cortlandt.

ROBESON RIOTS. Troop K troopers in this image are faced with one of their biggest challenges to date. More than 15,000 people, largely from New York City and Long Island, jammed the concert grounds of the old Hollowbrook Country Club in the town of Cortlandt to hear avowed communist and concert singer Paul Robeson on September 4, 1949. Opposed to the concert were some 5,000 anticommunist veterans from the Cortlandt and Peekskill area. Concert promoters were successful in staging a similar concert with Robeson performing in Peekskill at the Peekskill Stadium ball field in the summer of 1947. Though local veterans opposed it then, the fact that the 1949 concert was in the vicinity of four cemeteries that were actively being used to bury World War II service people at the time rallied the veterans against the insensitivity of the promoters. A huge protest march planned by local veterans groups ran a one-mile-long gauntlet, got out of control, and resulted in rioting. The infamous Robeson Riots became legendary in the Hudson Valley.

CHECKPOINT. Troopers set a checkpoint at Oregon Road (Hillside Avenue) and Locust Avenue in the town of Cortandt, one mile south of the concert grounds, preventing any vehicles from passing except those used to provide for the peaceful protest march planned by area veterans.

MOBILE COMMAND POST TRUCK. Troop K utilized the communication combination mobile command post truck for processing arrests and as a receiving point for confiscated weapons and other contraband. Shown are the numerous baseball bats taken from the swelling crowds.

STATE POLICE COMMAND POST. Troop K troopers set up a command post just north of the entrance to the concert grounds. They were assisted by numerous Westchester County police agencies. The police vehicles are parked on vacant farmland that is now mixed commercial and residential properties that are linked by Westbrook Drive.

PROTECTION FOR CONCERT SUPPORTERS. Capt. Daniel F. Glasheen and other state police personnel assist one of the concert promoters in entering the concert grounds safely.

PROTESTERS ARRESTED. Numerous agitators, who were opposed to the concert, were arrested by the state police in an attempt to curb the violence.

Arrest by Troop Commander. Capt. Daniel F. Glasheen personally takes a protester into custody. Police reported finding a knife in a sheath strapped to his ankle and apprehended the man before anyone was injured. Every member of Troop K and adjoining police agencies made every attempt at keeping the event peaceful.

ANTICOMMUNIST PROTESTERS. Over 5,000 veterans and anticommunist protesters massed in the Hollowbrook area of Cortlandt, at times overwhelming the police. The concert was held without any interruptions. It was only upon the completion of the program, after an impressive veterans parade had been disbanded and the marchers asked to leave, that violence flared. Scuffling between surging demonstrators and a small army of state troopers and deputized police officers preceded a rock barrage.

Paul Robeson. Two New York State troopers and a marine escort the main performer, Paul Robeson, riding in this black Buick sedan, safely onto the concert grounds. The performer also brought his own armed guards for protection from the protesters.

VETERANS PARADE. Over 3,500 persons, mostly veterans, participated in the patriotic parade and counter demonstration on Hillside Avenue, now called Oregon Road, in Cortlandt on Sunday afternoon, September 4, 1949. The parade protested the Robeson concert being staged on the grounds of the former Hollowbrook Country Club nearby. The parade started at 1:15 p.m., and at 3:20 p.m., the Veterans of Foreign Wars announced that the parade would be disbanded and urged all veterans to go home and cooperate with the authorities.

DAMAGE IN THE THOUSANDS. Vehicles were damaged and over 150 people were hurt as violence flared at the end of the concert. Demonstrators strung themselves along Hillside Avenue (Oregon Road) toward the city of Peekskill for nearly two miles and peppered the cars and buses with rocks and stones as the concertgoers sped away from the scene.

MASS HYSTERIA. As the concert ended in darkness and tempers flared, total chaos took hold. Counter charges from both sides were leveled about who instigated the riot. Cars and buses were stoned and some turned over. A collection of newspaper articles and pictures on the Robeson Riot made up part of a file used for study by the House of Representatives and Senate conferees of the 83rd Congress in preparation of the 1954 legislation to outlaw the Communist Party in the United States.

TROOPER THEODORE A. DOBBS. Between 1917 and 1949, 10 members of Troop K died as a result of injuries sustained in the line of duty. Theodore A. Dobbs entered the division on March 1, 1922. Trooper Dobbs was struck by a truck that had passed a stop sign and entered Jericho Turnpike in Mineola. Dobbs lost his leg to surgical amputation and later succumbed to infection and pneumonia.

TROOPER JOHN J. LANE. John J. Lane entered the division on April 1, 1927. Trooper Lane died on May 13, 1928, when he fell over a stairway rail and landed on his head at the Bay Shore barracks. Trooper Lane was interviewing an area patrolman at the station concerning vandalism to construction equipment on the Wantagh Parkway. The Bay Shore Station was located on the second floor of a storefront office, and when trooper Lane leaned against the banister, he lost his balance and fell to the ground. He died instantly from his injury.

CPL. EDWARD F. DOLPHIN. Edward F. Dolphin entered the division on April 15, 1924. Corporal Dolphin was injured when he was thrown from his police motorcycle after it struck a pothole in Valhalla on July 27, 1928. Corporal Dolphin died from his injuries on August 6, 1928.

TROOPER CARL T. WILDER. Carl T. Wilder entered the division on April 1, 1927. Trooper Wilder was shot and killed during a traffic stop on Tuxedo-Greenwood Lake Highway in the village of Tuxedo on September 7, 1928. No suspects were ever identified. Trooper Wilder was unable to reply to inquiries regarding his assailant before he died.

TROOPER GARLAND BLAIR. Garland Blair entered the division on July 15, 1930. Trooper Blair died on October 21, 1931, after the police vehicle he was traveling in overturned. Trooper Blair was returning from an investigation with another trooper, who was driving. To avoid a collision with a vehicle being operated on the wrong side of the road, the trooper swerved and the police vehicle overturned, killing trooper Blair.

TROOPER VINCENT A. DUNN. Vincent A. Dunn entered the division on May 1, 1927. Trooper Dunn died on September 30, 1932, in an automobile accident while returning to State Police Brewster.

Trooper Thomas C. Lynes. Thomas C. Lynes entered the division on July 16, 1933. Trooper Lynes died on June 3, 1935, when his automobile left the road, struck a sign, and crashed through trees into a gully on Route 9G in Dutchess County.

Trooper John G. Lord. John G. Lord entered the division on May 16, 1921. Trooper Lord died on July 23, 1935, when his patrol car struck the center isle of the Bronx River Parkway and flipped over twice during a heavy rainstorm.

TROOPER WILLIAM T. GRAYDON. William T. Graydon entered the division on July 1, 1936. Trooper Graydon died on March 19, 1938, when his car ran off the Bronx River Parkway and he was ejected from the vehicle.

TROOPER WILLIAM F. DOBBS JR. William F. Dobbs entered the division on August 16, 1936. Trooper Dobbs died on September 24, 1939, when his motorcycle struck a vehicle that had just been involved in an accident. He was thrown 15 feet and died from his injuries later that day.

EPILOGUE

Maj. George Fletcher Chandler did more than merely establish a police force for New York State. He also called his troopers, present and future, to lofty standards of behavior in dealing with people from all walks of life, especially with common, everyday folk. In his book, *The Policeman's Art*, Chandler drew upon the thoughts of a university professor as he held aloft these ideals:

> Professor William G. Sumner, of Yale, divided the people of the United States into four classes: A – The Rich Man, who has his money through inheritance, or has made it, whether honestly or dishonestly. B – The Poor Man, who, as a class, has little power. C – The reformer, who by stirring up existing conditions makes his own living. Lastly (the largest class of all), D – "The Forgotten Man." He is the every-day citizen, the voter, the taxpayer, who gets nothing from A, helps take care of B, and practically supports C; in fact, he carries the load of the nation on his shoulders.
>
> D, "The Forgotten Man," is the man whose servant the police should practically be. Let us treat him as we would wish to be treated ourselves, with courtesy, with fairness, and above all, with honesty. If he calls on us for service, give him immediate attention, no matter how trivial the request. It means much to him, little to us, but perhaps a great deal to our profession.
>
> I do not mean that we can not be of use to A, B and C. These classes are more prominent and naturally present themselves more frequently for our attention for service.
>
> But it is D, "The Forgotten Man," the average American, who represents the people as a whole. If we treat him fairly and make him like us, he and his kind will line up solidly behind us to preach the motto of the New York State Police: "Obedience to Law is Liberty."